Werewolves

by Grace Hansen

Abdo Kids
WORLD OF MYTHICAL BEINGS

Abdo Kids Jumbo is an Imprint of Abdo Kids
abdobooks.com

abdobooks.com

Published by Abdo Kids, a division of ABDO, P.O. Box 398166, Minneapolis, Minnesota 55439.

Printed in the United States of America, North Mankato, Minnesota.

052022

092022

THIS BOOK CONTAINS RECYCLED MATERIALS

Photo Credits: Alamy, Everette Collection, Getty Images, Granger Collection, Shutterstock

Production Contributors: Teddy Borth, Jennie Forsberg, Grace Hansen
Design Contributors: Candice Keimig, Pakou Moua

Library of Congress Control Number: 2021950567

Publisher's Cataloging-in-Publication Data

Names: Hansen, Grace, author.

Title: Werewolves / by Grace Hansen.

Description: Minneapolis, Minnesota : Abdo Kids, 2023 | Series: World of mythical beings | Includes online resources and index.

Identifiers: ISBN 9781098261924 (lib. bdg.) | ISBN 9781098262761 (ebook) | ISBN 9781098263188 (Read-to-Me ebook)

Subjects: LCSH: Werewolves--Juvenile literature. | Mythical animals--Juvenile literature. | Folklore--Juvenile literature. | Legends--Juvenile literature.

Classification: DDC 398.24--dc23

Table of Contents

Myth of the Werewolf

Werewolves are mythical creatures. They are humans that can turn into wolves. They are beastly and bloodthirsty.

The First Werewolves

Wolf-like creatures appeared in the ancient myths of Greece and Rome. Herodotus was a Greek writer. He wrote about a tribe called the **Neuri**. He said the people turned into wolves for a few days each year.

Herodotus

One Greek myth tells of the legend of Lycaon. King Lycaon is cruel and tries to trick Zeus, king of the gods. Zeus becomes so angry with King Lycaon that he turns the man into a wolf.

Medieval Europeans believed in werewolves. Even up until the 18th century, there were werewolf reports. People were **accused** of being werewolves. Others believed they were werewolves themselves.

In the mid-1700s, a town in France was being terrorized. A wolf-like creature was said to be attacking people. It added to the belief in werewolves.

Becoming a Werewolf

Different legends give different reasons for people changing into wolves. Drinking or touching the water a wolf has been in will transform a person. In France and Germany, legends said a full moon was to blame.

The most common way to turn into a werewolf is to be bitten by one. If the person survives the bite, they will become a werewolf too.

Some myths tell of people changing completely into wolves. Some say that a person will become half man, half wolf.

In some legends, a person can decide when they change. In others, the **cursed** human has no control. And once they are a werewolf, they create chaos and terror.

Modern Werewolves Based in Mythology

Jacob Black
Twilight series

- Can shapeshift into a giant wolf at will
- Based on some American Indian beliefs in shapeshifters

Rahne Sinclair
Marvel Comics

- Goes by the name Wolfsbane
- Can change into a wolf at will
- Has had to practice controlling her actions when she is in wolf form

Remus Lupin
Harry Potter series

- Bitten by a werewolf as a young child
- His transformation from human to werewolf, which happens once a month, is painful
- Cannot control his actions as a werewolf

Glossary

accused – to blame or charge with doing something wrong.

cursed – caused to suffer.

medieval – of or having to do with the Middle Ages.

Neuri – according to Herodotus, the Neuri were a nomadic tribe of magical men from Scythia, land that is now part of Russia.

Index